Key Battles of World War II

Fiona Reynoldson

www.heinemann.co.uk
Visit our website to find out more information about Heinemann Library books.

To order:
 Phone 44 (0) 1865 888066
 Send a fax to 44 (0) 1865 314091
Visit the Heinemann Bookshop at www.heinemann.co.uk to browse our catalogue and order online.

First published in Great Britain by Heinemann Library,
Halley Court, Jordan Hill, Oxford OX2 8EJ,
a division of Reed Educational and Professional Publishing Ltd.
Heinemann is a registered trademark of Reed Educational and Professional Publishing Ltd.

OXFORD   MELBOURNE   AUCKLAND
JOHANNESBURG   BLANTYRE   GABORONE
IBADAN   PORTSMOUTH (NH)   USA   CHICAGO

Designed by AMR
Illustrated by Art Construction
Originated by Dot Gradations
Printed by Wing King Tong in Hong Kong.

ISBN 0 431 11982 1 (hardback)   ISBN 0 431 11989 9 (paperback)
06 05 04 03 02   06 05 04 03 02
10 9 8 7 6 5 4 3 2   10 9 8 7 6 5 4 3 2 1

British Library Cataloguing in Publication Data
Reynoldson, Fiona
  Key battles of World War Two. – (20th century perspectives)
  1.World War, 1939–1945 – Campaigns – Juvenile literature
  I.Title
  940.5'4

Acknowledgements
The publishers would like to thank the following for permission to reproduce photographs:
AKG, p.27; Camera press, p.40, 41; Corbis, pp.17, 37, 38; e.t. archive, p.6; Hulton Getty, pp. 8, 12, 20, 42; Imperial War Museum, pp. 9,15; IWM/Camera press, pp.13, 19, 33, 35, 36; IWR/TRH pictures, p.23; IWR/Camera Press, p. 10; Novosti, pp.28, 29, 31; TRH Pictures, pp.5, 18, 22, 25, 26, 30, 39; TRH Pictures/Australian War Memorial, p. 43; TRH/IWM, p. 34.

Cover photograph reproduced with permission of Corbis.

Our thanks to Christopher Gibb, Alastair Gray and Lorna Gray for their help.

Every effort has been made to contact copyright holders of any material reproduced in this book. Any omissions will be rectified in subsequent printings if notice is given to the publishers.

Any words appearing in the text in bold, **like this**, are explained in the glossary.

Contents

The invasion of Poland 1939

By the summer of 1939, most people in Europe knew that war was inevitable. Hitler had demanded or taken more and more land around Germany. Britain and France had vowed to stand firm. If he turned to attack Poland, they would declare war.

The Poles were expecting an attack – they had soldiers stationed along the frontier. But when the invasion came, it was so fast and so furious that it was over in weeks. It was the shortest and most decisive of all the German campaigns in World War Two. The German plan was straightforward. Several armies would attack Poland in a pincer movement, closing at Warsaw, the Polish capital, then they would destroy the encircled Polish armies.

Poland, for its part, intended to hold the invaders long enough for the British and French to send soldiers to help. This proved to be impossible. Polish reserve soldiers were being called up to join their army units as the first German **panzers** rolled over the frontiers. At 4.45 a.m. on 1 September 1939, two German Army Groups moved as planned with nearly 2000 tanks, and in the air 2000 planes launched a massive air strike on all bases in Poland, including Warsaw. Most of the Polish Air Force was destroyed within two days – though it had damaged or destroyed about 500 German planes. Within a matter of hours, Poland's small navy was overcome, although three **destroyers** and two submarines managed to slip away and escape to Britain.

Despite poor Polish roads, the Germans advanced up to 25 kilometres on the

Northern and central Europe, September 1939. On 1 September Germany invaded Poland from the west and north. On 17 September, the Soviet Union invaded from the east. Poland was defeated within two weeks, and divided between Germany and the Soviet Union.

Key
- Germany by the end of '38
- Seized by Germans, March '39
- Seized by Hungary, March '39
- Dominated by Germans
- → German invasion 1 September '39
- → USSR invasion 17 September '39

FINLAND

NORWAY

SWEDEN

ESTONIA

LATVIA

LITHUANIA

Baltic Sea

USSR

Berlin

GERMANY

Warsaw

POLAND

CZECHOSLOVAKIA

AUSTRIA

HUNGARY

ROMANIA

0   200 km
0   200 miles

first day. By 7 September they were within 65 kilometres of Warsaw. The Polish government had left the city the day before. As the Germans advanced, the Russians saw their opportunity and invaded Poland from the east. To the surprise and dismay of Britain and France, **fascist** Germany had made a treaty with **communist** Russia in August 1939. The two nations were supposed to be hated rivals. One of the secret clauses of the **treaty** was that they would carve up Poland between them. However, the Russians too were surprised by the speed of the German advance and did not want Germany to take over all of Poland.

These Stuka bombers were part of Germany's 'lightning war' (or Blitzkrieg) attack on Poland in September 1939.

Blitzkrieg – lightning war

The invasion of Poland was the first example of the German **Blitzkrieg**, or 'lightning war'. Blitzkrieg made use of fast-moving tanks and armoured vehicles, supported by aircraft. These forces could penetrate quickly deep behind enemy defences, and then circle round and destroy the enemy army. Poland and the rest of the world were taken by surprise. This would happen again and again in the early days of the war. It was at this point that Britain and France declared war on Germany, so spreading the fighting across Western Europe, and setting the scene for the rest of the war.

WHAT HAPPENED TO THE POLISH ARMY	
TAKEN PRISONER BY GERMANS	ABOUT 600,000
ESCAPED, MANY TO FIGHT WITH **ALLIES**	100,000

How had the war come about?

World War One ended in 1918. It was called the war to end all wars. Over seven million men had died. The vast majority of people did not ever want to fight another war. The victorious **Allies** decided to create the League of Nations. Over 50 countries joined it, but the USA did not. In theory, if one country was attacked, all the others would band together and refuse to trade with the attacker. This would mean there would be no more wars. However, if countries really wanted to fight, they did so. The League of Nations was like a lion with no teeth.

The Nazis were excellent at propaganda. This 1923 election poster reads: 'Workers of the brow and of the fist, vote for Hitler, the front-line soldier.'

Peace or armistice?

'This is not a peace treaty, it is an armistice [ceasefire] for twenty years.'

The Allied commander-in-chief, Marshal Foch's comment on the terms of the Treaty of Versailles 1919

ARBEITER

DER STIRN
DER FAUST

WÄHLT DEN FRONTSOLDATEN

HITLER!

The aftermath of World War One

After World War One, Germany was devastated. Under the **Treaty of Versailles**, the victorious Allies made sure that Germany lost land, that it was only allowed a small army and no navy or airforce, and that it paid large sums of money for damage done during the war.

The rise of Hitler and the Nazis

The large sums of money that Germany had to pay for the war damage were called **reparations**. France was particularly keen on reparations because so much of northern France had been destroyed by four years of war. Germany hated the reparations. Many Germans saw them as a symbol of the fact that their country was given all the blame for starting World War One. They also felt that they should never have lost the war and that somehow they were betrayed into surrender. When the future German leader Adolf Hitler appeared on the scene in the 1920s, he promised to make Germany rich and great again. He joined and then took over the Nationalist Socialist German Workers Party, which became known as the Nazi Party.

The Wall Street Crash and worldwide depression

The Wall Street Crash on the American **stock market** in 1929 affected countries all over the world, leading to widespread unemployment. It became known as the Great Depression. In Germany Hitler said he would create jobs and he would make businesses work. In 1933 he was elected **chancellor**, and shortly afterwards began to call himself Führer (leader) of Germany.

The road to war

After 1933 there were more jobs in Germany. However, there were more jobs in other countries too. The world had begun to pull out of the worst of the Depression, though Hitler took the credit for saving Germany. At the same time he was determined to avenge Germany's defeat in World War One. He started to build up an army again and to demand German land back.

Other countries were nervous about this but no one wanted another war. Britain felt that Germany should be treated better. In 1936, when German soldiers marched into the Ruhr – an important industrial district – and took it back from France, no one really protested. This was followed by the German invasion of Austria in 1938 and the demand for part of **Czechoslovakia**. The British and French agreed because nearly all the people in that part of Czechoslovakia were German. This agreement was signed in Munich. The policy of saying yes to Hitler's demands was called **appeasement**.

Within months Hitler wanted more of Czechoslovakia. It was obvious that war was coming. Hitler had stated that he wanted more **Lebensraum** ('living space') for the German people in the East, and he was not going to stop unless he was made to. On 1 September 1939, after securing his back with a **treaty** with Stalin's Russia, Germany invaded Poland in the lightning attack, or **Blitzkrieg**, which stunned the rest of the world by its sheer speed. (See map on page 4).

Blitzkrieg goes west 1940

After the invasion of Poland in September 1939 very little happened for months. This became known as the 'phoney war'. Then in April 1940, Germany invaded Denmark and Norway and followed this by invading the Netherlands and Belgium, which was neutral.

The German attack

The German attack began on 10 May and the Netherlands was overwhelmed in a few days while the main German army moved on to Belgium. The Belgians fought bravely but the Germans were already attacking from the north through the now conquered Netherlands as well as from the east. **Paratroopers** were dropped at key points, and at rivers a combination of **dive bombers** and armoured vehicles often panicked the soldiers defending the crossings. At the fortress of Eben Emael, German **glider troops** landed on the roof and blasted their way inside, forcing the Belgian soldiers to surrender. French and British soldiers committed to help the Belgians fell back before the German onslaught.

The German advance in May 1940 forced British and French troops back to Dunkirk.

Key
→ German advance
— Maginot Line

Why were the Germans so successful?

The Germans had about the same number of soldiers and tanks as the **Allies** (the French, British, Belgians and Dutch), though they had more aeroplanes. However, the Allies were a mixture of nationalities and abilities, and they were facing a very well-organized army and airforce whose leaders had planned and practised the whole of the attack, which they called Operation Sicklestroke. Their tanks were organized into ten **panzer** divisions and worked closely with the airforce, as they had done in Poland. The Germans had a very clear idea of what they wanted to do, while the Allies were simply defending. Added to this the ordinary soldier was not very keen on the war. Germany was fired up for war, while the Allies were not.

The fall of France

By mid-May the Germans were bursting through the hilly forests of the Ardennes and into France. The French had always assumed that tanks and other vehicles could not get through the Ardennes so they had left it almost undefended. Instead after World War One they had spent eight years building the vast **Maginot Line** to the south to stop Germany ever being able to invade. The German army just went round it.

The retreat to Britain

On 28 May the Belgians finally surrendered, by which time the British and many of the French had been forced back to Dunkirk, where they were encircled by the Germans. However, Hitler halted his army so that they could regroup before their final victory. This gave the British a two-day breathing space. On 27 May the Royal Navy started to **evacuate** soldiers from the Dunkirk beaches.

Thousands and thousands of Allied soldiers lined the beaches. The big ships often had to stand well off shore while smaller boats ferried the soldiers from the beaches. Everything was left behind except the clothes the soldiers stood up in and their rifles. Sometimes even their coats were left in the sea as they waded out to the boats. The German airforce bombed the beaches but most of the bombs plunged into the soft sand and did little harm. By 4 June, the evacuation stopped. The Germans broke through but 338,226 men had been rescued, a third of them French. The British army had lost all its tanks, guns and lorries, but at least it lived to fight another day.

No one knew how soon that day might be. In fact Hitler intended to follow up the defeat of France with the invasion of Britain. The key battle would be the Battle of Britain.

This painting by war artist Charles Chundall shows the dramatic rescue of Allied troops from Dunkirk. Smaller boats ferry soldiers out to the waiting troop ships, while the German army bombs the beaches.

Operation Dynamo

Operation Dynamo was the code name for the Dunkirk evacuation. It was hoped that the navy could rescue 35,000 soldiers. In the event the rescue lasted nine days and brought ten times that number of men back to England. The government ordered that any boats in southern England over 30 m long had to take part. Naval officers were put in charge, but civilian crews endangered their own lives by making repeated trips to help with the evacuation.

The Battle of Britain 1940

In July 1940, Hitler gave orders for the preparation of a seaborne invasion of Britain, called Operation Sealion. However, first he had to destroy the Royal Air Force (RAF) so that it could not bomb the German invasion ships as they sailed for Britain.

On 10 July the **Luftwaffe** (German airforce) made their first bomber attack on British ships in the Channel. However, using their new **radar** equipment, the British detected the bombers and sent four squadrons of British fighters to drive them off. This was the beginning of the Battle of Britain.

A long hot summer

It was a beautiful summer. Day after day the clear blue skies over the coast and countryside of south-east England were the scene of desperate battles between German and British planes. The German bombers headed for the RAF airfields. The slow, heavy bombers were escorted by fighter planes such as the very fast Messerschmitt 109. The RAF fighter planes were mainly Hurricanes and Spitfires. They were not as fast as the Messerschmitts but they were quicker to turn. This was important in the twisting and turning dogfights in the skies.

Other things helped in the battle too. Air Chief Marshal Dowding was head of RAF Fighter Command. He made use of the new invention of radar. The radar stations picked up German bombers on their screens as

RAF pilots run to their planes during the Battle of Britain in the summer of 1940. At the height of the battle, pilots were making as many as seven sorties a day.

they were flying over the English Channel. In addition, the Observer Corps was made up of people who were on duty watching for German planes all along the south part of Britain. By using new land-to-air radio, which the Germans did not have, RAF fighter planes were told where the German bombers were.

On 15 August the Germans made their biggest attack of the battle so far. Fighting went on all day. By now the British were becoming anxious about the supply of pilots and fighter planes. There were few planes or pilots in reserve. Pilots were flying up to seven **sorties** a day and snatching sleep when they could. Then, on 7 September, the Germans switched to bombing London.

The final battle

On 15 September a desperate battle took place over London. The *Luftwaffe* flew in vast numbers. The RAF were forced to use all the planes they had. There were no reserves. The fighting went on all day and at the end the Germans had lost more planes than the British had.

The Battle of Britain was over. From then on, the Germans switched their attack to bombing British cities.

The Battle of Britain marked the limits of German expansion in the West and showed the world that the German forces could be stopped.

Frank Webster was a Spitfire pilot in the Battle of Britain, flying with 610 Squadron. He was shot down and killed on 26 August 1940. Frank is wearing a flying suit and fur-lined boots. Fighter pilots often cut off the fur collar so they could turn their heads easily and spot enemy planes approaching.

WHO FOUGHT IN THE BATTLE OF BRITAIN?
NATIONALITIES OF PILOTS FLYING WITH THE RAF IN THE BATTLE OF BRITAIN

UNITED KINGDOM	2429
POLISH	141
NEW ZEALAND	102
CANADIAN	90
CZECHOSLOVAK	86
BELGIAN	29
AUSTRALIAN	21
SOUTH AFRICAN	21
FRENCH	13
AMERICAN	7
RHODESIAN	2
OTHERS	11
RAF PILOTS KILLED	510

The Battle of the Atlantic 1940–43

If Britain was going to hold out against the Germans it would need guns, aeroplanes, ships, tanks, oil and food. All these were in short supply in 1940. At this time, Britain only produced one third of the food it needed to feed its population. The rest came to Britain from other countries by sea. The desperate struggle to bring food and other goods to Britain cost thousands of lives and ships, as Germany tried to cut off essential supplies. The main supply route was across the Atlantic Ocean from the USA. At first the **U-boats** (German submarines) attacked the merchant ships in the Western Approaches as they were reaching Britain. However, by 1940, this area was well patrolled by the British and the U-boats moved further out into the Atlantic Ocean.

The Atlantic Gap

The major problem facing the **Allies** in protecting the merchant ships from German attack was that vast stretches of the Atlantic could not be patrolled by air. At this time, planes could only fly a few hundred kilometres before they had to return to base to be refuelled. This left the merchant ships unprotected for a large part of the ocean, known as the Atlantic Gap. The Allies did not have enough escort vessels. Until early 1941, the U-boats were very successful.

A US Navy flying boat watches over a huge convoy of supply ships in the North Atlantic in November 1941. These planes played an important role in keeping the sea routes open.

Allied convoys

Many of the German submarines were based on the west coast of France. From there groups ('wolf packs') of U-boats went out to hunt the Allied **convoys**. A typical convoy consisted of 40 to 50 merchant ships sailing in columns to form a box shape. A small number of escort ships patrolled the edges of the convoy. In conditions ranging from sunny, calm weather with a gentle swell to violent, gale-force winds with waves metres high, the convoy would move slowly towards Britain from America.

German submarine wolf packs

The wolf packs often waited, half submerged, ahead of the convoy, ready to attack. The escort ships could only detect submarines for about one kilometre using Asdic (a device using sound waves underwater).

With few escort ships it was easy for U-boats to sneak through and massacre a convoy, so that in 1941, one in four ships sailing to Britain was sunk.

However, once one of the submarines launched its torpedoes, the naval escort ships set out to hunt the submarine. Apart from Asdic, they used **radar** to detect any submarines on the surface and listening devices to 'hear' the submarine engines and propellers beneath the surface. Once detected, the escort ship used underwater bombs called depth charges thrown out from the back of the ship. These were set to explode at different depths and often in patterns to cover the area in which the submarine was probably lurking.

A German U-boat on the surface.

As the Battle of the Atlantic progressed, the Allies totalled the monthly tonnage of merchant ships and their cargoes that had been sunk against the number of submarines sunk. The Germans did similar calculations. From 1943, the trend began to go against the Germans, with more and more submarines sunk. This turning point was brought about by the larger numbers of escort ships covering each convoy, the increasing range of aircraft and the introduction of small aircraft carriers for planes to fly from. All this closed the Atlantic Gap and made it increasingly difficult for the German submarines to go undetected.

Bringing troops

Men as well as goods had to be brought across the Atlantic to fight in Europe. The *Queen Mary* and the *Queen Elizabeth* were two of the biggest passenger liners ever built. In peacetime they carried about 2000 passengers and over 1000 officers and crew. In wartime, they carried 15,000 soldiers from Canada and the US on each trip. The liners were so fast that they travelled alone because no U-boat could catch up with them.

A world war

The trading links between Britain and America were vital to enable Britain to maintain its fight against Germany throughout 1940 and 1941.

Meanwhile, there were changes on the opposite side of the world. Japan was emerging as a powerful nation. By 1931, Japan had gained land in northern China. In 1937 it had invaded more of mainland China, capturing all the important cities and ports. Now the Japanese could ship coal and iron ore from China to Japan to feed the heavy industries needed to make machines, ships, aeroplanes and tanks.

The all-out war on China had been watched by many foreign observers. It had led to mounting tension between the USA and Japan. Nor were relations between Japan and Britain any better. Japan aimed to cut China's trade routes to the outside world and this affected Britain. In 1940 the Japanese succeeded in closing the Burma Road – which led from south-west China to British-held Burma – for a few months. This road was important because it linked the Nationalist Chinese forces with the British Empire.

This soldier was in close combat for many hours. The tension of fear and of concentration exhausted him so he could not close his jaw or focus his eyes. Later in the war, the US Marines called this 'the 2000 yard stare'. It was typical of soldiers fighting on any side in the war.

The Soviet Union and Japan

Then in 1941 the Japanese signed a non-aggression pact – an agreement that neither country would attack the other – with the Soviet Union. This was very important to Japan, who could not expand in the Pacific if there was any risk of the the Soviet Union attacking while its back was turned. It also suited the Soviet Union, who were facing Nazi Germany on their western front and could not afford a conflict with Japan in the east. (See map on page 16).

The French, the Dutch, the USA and Japan

In July 1941 Japanese soldiers invaded French **Indo-China** with a view to taking the Dutch **East Indies**. Both France and the Netherlands had been occupied by the Germans in 1940 and could not defend their **colonies**. The oil-rich Dutch East Indies were particularly important to Japan. The campaign in China was draining Japanese oil reserves. This was extremely serious because 80 per cent of Japan's oil came from the USA, who was becoming increasingly unfriendly to Japan.

Breaking off trading relations

The invasion of French Indo-China meant that Japanese bombers and ships were within easy striking distance of the Dutch East Indies. Horrified, the American, British and Dutch governments cut all trading links with Japan. Negotiations dragged on through the summer and autumn, but neither Japan nor the USA would make any real concessions.

Japan's options

By October, Japan had decided to establish the Greater East Asia Co-Prosperity Sphere (in many ways a Japanese empire). The head of the Japanese government, General Hideki Tojo, announced that 'the Japanese empire stands at the cross-roads of its rise or fall.' It was obvious that any increase in the size of the Japanese empire would clash with US, British, French and Dutch interests and might threaten Australia. Given the war in Europe, the USA was the only power that could put a stop to Japan. The Japanese were only too well aware of this, and decided on a **pre-emptive** strike. They would destroy the US Pacific Fleet, thereby taking out their main rival.

INDIE MOET VRIJ !
WERKT EN VECHT ERVOOR !

This Dutch poster shows the Greater East Asia Co-Prosperity Sphere as an octopus, reaching its tentacles out across the Dutch East Indies.

PLANNING FOR PEARL HARBOR

PLANNING FOR AN ATTACK ON THE US BASE AT PEARL HARBOR STARTED IN JANUARY 1941. IN NOVEMBER, THIS IS THE JAPANESE FORCE THAT SET SAIL:

6 AIRCRAFT CARRIERS	3 SUBMARINES
2 BATTLESHIPS	8 OIL TANKERS
3 CRUISERS	1 SUPPLY SHIP
9 DESTROYERS	

Pearl Harbor 1941

After the bombing of Pearl Harbor the Japanese conquered more and more of south-east Asia.

Japan lies in the West Pacific Ocean. For some years relations between the USA and Japan had been strained. Both countries had trading interests around the Pacific Ocean. The Japanese in particular wanted to expand their trade and empire. The Americans wanted to protect their trade. They eventually reacted by cutting off supplies of oil to Japan. This was a great blow to the Japanese. They had little oil or raw materials of their own. They had to either give in to American pressure or fight. They decided to fight.

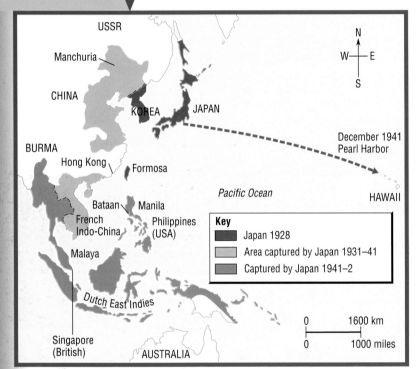

The Japanese knew that if they invaded more islands in the western Pacific (particularly oil-rich islands) the USA would react strongly. So the Japanese decided on a **pre-emptive** strike. They would destroy the big American naval base at Pearl Harbor in Hawaii. Then, with no warships left, the Americans could not stop the Japanese from taking more islands.

A silent approach

On 26 November 1941, the Japanese secretly set sail for Pearl Harbor. They sailed far to the north of the usual shipping lanes so they would not meet other ships. On the night of 6 December, they silently closed in on Pearl Harbor.

It was a beautiful Saturday night. The Japanese sailors tuned their radios to the American stations and listened to dance band music while they waited.

There were 92 American ships in Pearl Harbor, including eight big battleships. This was unusual. Normally half the battleships were out on patrol, but because they were slow and easily bombed by aeroplanes, the American navy was nervous. They knew the Japanese were thinking of war, so the battleships were only allowed out with aircraft carriers to escort them. It just so happened that two aircraft carriers were out. They were ferrying aeroplanes to other islands in the Pacific Ocean, so the battleships stayed in.

Taken by surprise

On the morning of 7 December, a Japanese submarine sneaked into Pearl Harbor. It was blown up, but where had it come from and why? Then at 7.02 a.m., two **radar** operators saw a blip on the radar screen that meant many aeroplanes approaching fast. They phoned headquarters and were told not to worry. Some American planes were due to arrive. It must be them. The radar operators went off to breakfast.

At 7.55 a.m. Mitsuo Fuchida led the Japanese planes in to bomb Pearl Harbor. The Americans could not believe it was happening. There were shattering roars and billowing clouds of smoke as torpedoes slammed into the ships. Sailors tumbled from their bunks and ran to the guns as ships caught fire and started to sink. Then the Japanese pilots turned their attention to the seven airfields. The American planes were all parked neatly together. Most of the planes were destroyed or damaged. Later in the war, planes were always dispersed around the airfield so that they would not be such a sitting target.

By 10.00 a.m. the bombing was over. The best of the American battleships had been sunk or badly damaged; many Americans had been wounded or killed. The Japanese flew back to their aircraft carriers while the dazed Americans started to clear up.

The destruction of Pearl Harbor. This photograph shows the USS Shaw being blown up.

A triumph for Japan?

So what were the results of this one-sided battle? The Japanese were triumphant. They went on to take island after island in the Pacific Ocean for several months, while it took the Americans months to recover. However, the bombing of Pearl Harbor brought the USA into the war on the Allied side, alongside Britain, against Japan and Germany. From now on the war became truly a world war, fought all over the globe. Moreover, the American aircraft carriers had escaped. They lived to fight another day and to change the way in which sea battles were fought.

17

n the Far East 1942

he Japanese invasion of Malaya

mmediately after their triumph at Pearl Harbor, the Japanese invaded e British **colony** of Malaya on 8 December 1941. The British were fighting for their survival in Europe. They had few troops in Malaya, and far fewer aeroplanes than the Japanese and they underestimated Japanese fighting capacities. A British battleship, the *Prince of Wales* and the battle cruiser *Repulse*, had been sunk. The British fought hard, but were overwhelmed and retreated through the jungle towards Singapore. The Japanese soldiers were better jungle fighters and they also used bicycles and tanks to speed up their advance along the jungle tracks. By 31 January, the British had retreated to Singapore at the tip of Malaya.

The invasion of Singapore

Singapore is a diamond-shaped island, 42 kilometres long and 22 kilometres wide, at the foot of the Malaya **peninsula** (see map on page 16). In 1941 it had a busy port. There were guns defending the port but these faced the sea. The British had expected to hold Malaya so they had not expected to defend Singapore from the north. There were about 80,000 soldiers on the island, including Australian, Malay, Indian and British troops. As the Japanese got nearer they began bombing the island. By the beginning of February they were close to Singapore itself. They landed a total of three divisions of soldiers. Soon they captured the three reservoirs on the island. The British surrendered and thousands of soldiers became prisoners of war without ever having fired a shot. Singapore was surrendered to the Japanese on 15 February 1942. Defeats like this weakened the British empire, and after the war it began to break up.

General Percival surrendering the British flag to the Japanese at Singapore.

The Japanese invasion of the Philippines

The U.S. commander, Lt. General Douglas MacArthur had said that he could prevent a Japanese invasion anywhere on the Philippines. However, on 8 December, within ten hours of devastating the U.S. Pacific Fleet at Pearl Harbor, the Japanese began landing troops throughout the Philippine Islands. (See map on page 16).

American soldiers on the notorious Bataan death march.

They also attacked the American airfields at Formosa (now Taiwan) where they destroyed 103 aircraft, ensuring air superiority for the rest of the campaign. In December, MacArthur had to abandon the capital Manila, and was then forced to retreat to the Bataan Peninsula.

The invasion of the Philippines had been so easy that the Japanese withdrew some forces to attack the nearby Dutch **East Indies**. When they fell on 22 February 1942, the Japanese troops returned to Bataan and the American forces there surrendered on 8 April 1942. When President Roosevelt had ordered MacArthur to Australia in March 1942, he vowed 'I will return'– which he did in 1944.

Corregidor and surrender

The Japanese then attacked the near-by island of Corregidor in Manila Bay. In one month they took this fortress from the Americans. The Japanese terms of surrender of 7 May 1942 included the surrender of all the Philippines to them.

Bataan Death March 10–22 April 1942

More than 70,000 Americans and Filipinos were captured and forced to march 105 km to Camp O'Donnell. They were beaten and starved and many who fell from exhaustion were killed. Probably 7000–10,000 died on the march and as many escaped into the surrounding jungle. After the war the Japanese commander, General Masaharu Homma was tried and executed for his responsibility for the Bataan Death March, although he had been more lenient than his superiors wished.

The Battle of Coral Sea 1942

After Pearl Harbor, the Japanese took more and more islands in the Western Pacific Ocean. Neither the Americans nor the British could stop them.

In May 1942 the Japanese planned to invade Port Moresby. As far as the **Allies** were concerned, this was dangerously close to Australia and New Zealand. Yet what could they do? The Japanese seemed to be unstoppable.

The US aircraft carrier USS Enterprise. Aircraft carriers had crews of up to 3000 men, including sailors, airmen, mechanics, cooks and bakers.

But the USA had three advantages. First, they had three aircraft carriers in the Western Pacific. Two were the carriers that had been saved because they were out delivering aeroplanes when the Japanese bombed Pearl Harbor. Also the Americans had broken the Japanese codes before the war so they could decipher many of their enemy's naval messages. By mid April 1942, the Americans knew that the Japanese were planning to invade Port Moresby with a view to bombing Australia from there. Third, the Japanese had severely damaged the American battleship fleet at Pearl Harbor. So the Americans were forced to adopt a new type of warfare, using aircraft carriers and aeroplanes instead of battleships.

The battle

By early May the combined American and Australian fleet was in the Coral Sea, off Australia. So was the Japanese fleet. They each sent planes out and had a good idea of where each other's ships were, despite rain and bad weather. Some bombing went on and each side lost planes and ships.

On 8 May the battle reached a crisis. Each side had two aircraft carriers and about the same number of planes and smaller ships. At dawn both sides sent out planes despite heavy rain. Throughout the day the planes bombed and torpedoed the enemy's ships.

By the afternoon, the US carrier, the *Lexington*, had fires raging out of control. By 5 p.m., the orders were given to abandon ship. The other American carrier, *Yorktown*, was damaged. On the Japanese side, one carrier was sunk and one destroyed. So the battle was a draw, but two things made it a very important battle. It stopped the Japanese from invading Port Moresby and threatening Australia. It was also the first sea battle in history when the opposing sides' ships never so much as caught sight of each other.

This map shows how close the Battle of Coral Sea was to Australia.

The plane that sunk the Lexington:

The Nakajima B5N2 'Kate'. This Japanese plane was in the forefront of the Pearl Harbor attack and later was involved in the sinking of the *Lexington*, *Yorktown* and *Hornet*. Maximum speed: 380 kph at 3600 metres. Maximum range: 1990 kilometres. Armament: 1, 7.7 mm machine-gun plus 800 kg of bombs or torpedoes.

The Battle of Midway 1942

Admiral Isoroku Yamamoto was commander-in-chief of the Japanese Combined Fleet. He never wanted war with the USA. He was worried about Japan's ability to fight the USA in a long war. Having lived and worked in the USA he knew its industrial might. The USA was a rich, powerful country with enormous industries. Yamamoto knew that in a year or so the USA could turn its factories over to making so many ships, guns and aeroplanes that Japan might be overwhelmed. Therefore the Japanese had to completely destroy the US Pacific Fleet as soon as possible. Only then could they hope to dominate the Pacific Ocean and perhaps come to some peaceful agreement with the USA.

On board a US Navy aircraft carrier. The crew are preparing for a raid.

So Yamamoto planned the destruction of the American fleet at Midway Island. Midway was in fact two tiny islands almost surrounded by a coral reef. There was a harbour and an airfield.

The plan

Yamamoto made a complicated plan. Part of the Japanese navy would invade the Aleutian Islands far to the north. While the Americans rushed north to retake the Aleutians, another Japanese force would take Midway. The American fleet would rush back to Midway and then the Japanese fleet would blast it from the water.

However, the Americans could read the Japanese codes. They knew their enemy's plan so they sailed their fleet to Midway and waited.

The beginning of the battle

That whole area of the Pacific Ocean always has a lot of fog and rain in May and June, so it was difficult for searching planes to spot ships down below. The Japanese were not expecting the American fleet so they concentrated on attacking the island of Midway. They were shocked when at 7.30 a.m. a plane reported seeing about ten ships. The battle was on and raged all day as aeroplanes attacked ships on each side.

By 5 p.m. the American carrier *Yorktown* was finally sunk. But this was the only carrier the Americans lost, whereas the Japanese lost four aircraft carriers and twice as many aeroplanes. As night fell both sides drew away from each other. This time the Americans had undoubtedly won. The Battle of Midway was probably the most important battle of the Pacific War and a key turning point. Yamamoto knew that the Japanese could not make more and more aircraft carriers, whereas the Americans were now geared up for war and could easily replace their losses. From this time on the Japanese never won a major battle and the Americans, despite some set-backs, never lost, as they moved slowly across the Pacific Ocean towards Japan.

During the Battle of Midway a Japanese torpedo scored a direct hit on the American aircraft carrier, the USS Yorktown.

USS *Hornet*

One of the three US aircraft carriers at Midway was the USS *Hornet*. The *Hornet* was a 17,960-tonne carrier built in 1941. It had a crew of 2919. During the Battle of Midway, it was Avenger planes from the *Hornet* that helped destroy two Japanese aircraft carriers. However, the *Hornet* was severely damaged and was later sunk during the Battle of Santa Cruz.

Hitler and Stalin

Japan could concentrate on the war in the Pacific without fear of attack by the Soviet Union. From June 1941, the Soviet Union was at war with Germany in a struggle that lasted for four years. Only after May 1945 did the Soviets turn eastward and join with the Allied forces against Japan.

The Soviet-German non-aggression pact, August 1939

Before World War Two started, Hitler and Stalin had signed a non-aggression pact. This agreement shook the rest of the world. Hitler was fanatically anti-**communist**, yet he was signing an agreement with Stalin, the leader of the communist Soviet Union. The reason for their pact was that Hitler wanted to invade Poland without warlike objections from the Soviet Union. Stalin, for his part, knew that Hitler had no love for the Soviet Union and would attack if, and when, it suited him. The non-aggression pact bought time for the Soviet Union – time to move more factories hundreds of kilometres to the east, beyond the Ural Mountains, beyond the reach of a rapid German attack, and time to produce more war goods and recruit and train more soldiers. It also gave them an excuse to occupy half of Poland and the Baltic states of Lithuania, Latvia and Estonia. (See map on page 4.)

Operation Barbarossa – the German attack on the Soviet Union, 1941–42.

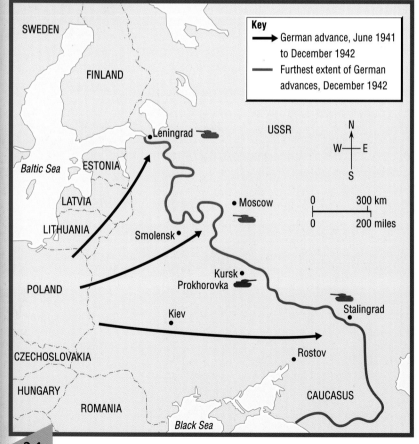

Key
→ German advance, June 1941 to December 1942
— Furthest extent of German advances, December 1942

SWEDEN
FINLAND
Baltic Sea
ESTONIA
LATVIA
LITHUANIA
POLAND
CZECHOSLOVAKIA
HUNGARY
ROMANIA
Black Sea
Leningrad
USSR
Moscow
Smolensk
Kursk
Prokhorovka
Kiev
Stalingrad
Rostov
CAUCASUS

N
W — E
S

0   300 km
0   200 miles

From Russia to the Soviet Union

Although Russia was a large country, it had suffered enormous upheavals since 1900. First, it had tried to catch up with the industrialized countries. Then it had been beset by World War One and the **Bolshevik** Revolution, which had overthrown the **tsar** and set up a communist government. In 1922 it became the Soviet Union. Several years of civil war were followed by many more years of disruption, as farms and factories changed over to being run on communist lines. All this, under Joseph

Stalin's harsh leadership, and the loss of millions of lives, had taken its toll on the country.

Operation Barbarossa, 22 June 1941

In fact, the non-aggression pact bought Stalin just over eighteen months. By the end of 1940, German advances in the west were halted by the Battle of Britain. Hitler turned east. On 22 June 1941, he invaded the Soviet Union in an attack codenamed Operation Barbarossa. Hitler's desire for **Lebensraum** (living space) for the German people was to be satisfied by taking land from Russia. However, by this time Hitler seemed to be behaving like the French Emperor Napoleon. In 1812, Napoleon had felt himself so powerful that he could take on Russia, and he set out for Moscow with a huge army. Like Napoleon, Hitler's army advanced rapidly at first, driving deep into the Soviet Union. Could this success last?

German advance 1941. The 148 invading German divisions inflicted massive defeats on the Soviet Army.

Britain or the Soviet Union?

Hitler did order preparations to be made for an invasion of England, but he was always half-hearted in his desire to launch a large seaborne landing. Germany, unlike Britain, was not a sea power.... And there was another ideological reason why Hitler was not fully committed to invading Britain. For him, it would have been a distraction. Britain contained neither the space, nor the raw materials, that he believed the new German Empire needed. And he admired the British.... If the Germans let themselves be drawn into a risky amphibious operation against a country Hitler had never wanted as an enemy, every day the potential threat from his greatest ideological opponent would be growing stronger.... All this meant that, from Hitler's point of view, there was an alternative to invading Britain: he could invade the Soviet Union.

from *War of the Century* by Laurence Rees, BBC 1999

Moscow 1941–42

At 3.15 a.m. on 22 June 1941, a huge German army launched an attack on the Soviet Union. This was called Operation Barbarossa. Armies of more than three million men on either side faced each other on the German-Soviet frontiers. The area over which they might be fighting was the size of half of Europe.

The Germans knew that they had to strike quickly. They had to defeat the Soviet Union before its soldiers could retreat into the vast Russian lands to the east; and they had to do it before the onset of winter. There were three main thrusts. One was in the north, towards Leningrad. One was in the centre towards Moscow, the capital of the Soviet Union, and the third was in the south towards the Ukraine.

German soldiers advancing into the Soviet Union.

Invasion

The German armoured divisions drove forward, covering 30 or more kilometres a day. In the first weeks of the war they encircled the Russian armies and took hundreds of thousands of prisoners. By 17 July, the German army was 500–800 kilometres inside Russia. However, the armoured divisions were outrunning their supplies and the infantry soldiers behind them could not keep up. Instead of capturing Moscow quickly, the armoured divisions had to wait around, sometimes for weeks, for ammunition, fuel and other supplies. They were losing valuable time.

The beginnings of winter, 1941–1942

By 30 October the German advance had come to a halt about a hundred kilometres west of Moscow. The Russian soldiers had been forced to retreat, but now they were fighting harder, helped by the wet autumn weather that bogged down the German trucks. Then, as the winter came, the roads started to freeze over and the Germans could move again. However, now the German soldiers did not have thick enough clothing for the severe Russian winter. Even to go outside without thick gloves on could mean frostbite in a few minutes. Moreover, the Germans found that the oil froze solid in their trucks, guns and other machinery. Both these things helped the Russians in the desperate defence of their capital city.

The Soviet plan

Other things helped the Russians too. Stalin, the Russian leader, was a ruthless dictator. Before the war he had been worried that some of the army generals might become too powerful, so he had had many of them killed. The Germans knew this and they assumed that there were no good Russian generals left. The Germans were confident they could defeat such a poor army. They also thought the Russians would run out of guns, tanks and all other machinery because so many factories had been destroyed in the German invasion. However, Stalin had planned for this. He had built hundreds of factories far to the east of Moscow, beyond the Ural mountains. These factories went on producing everything from tanks to rifles, far from the invading German army. The Russians did not only move their factories – all sorts of national treasures from museums and galleries were packed up and moved east. Also, to the surprise of the Germans, the Russian army did not collapse. It threw itself into defending the capital.

The German tanks moved further and further east, across the vast and empty Russian landscape.

The Battle for Moscow, 1941–1942

Three weeks before Christmas 1941, in the depths of the icy winter, the Russians counter-attacked. The Germans held on, but by spring 1942, as the weather improved, there was a stalemate. Neither side was winning. This was the first time in nearly nine months that the Germans had been halted in their headlong invasion of the Soviet Union. It showed the Russians that the Germans could be stopped and that Moscow could be saved. Just as the Battle of Britain was the point at which the German forces were stopped in the West, so the Battle of Moscow was the point at which they were stopped in the East.

The world map on pages 44–45 shows the Soviet Union and Moscow.

MEN AND TANKS AT THE BATTLE OF MOSCOW		
	SOLDIERS	TANKS
GERMAN	900,000	1600
SOVIET	950,000	1000

Stalingrad 1942

In July 1942, Hitler decided to leave the northern and central German armies to sit tight around Leningrad and Moscow because they were in a stalemate position. The northern German army had reached the outskirts of Leningrad (now St Petersburg) by 8 September 1941, but they could not breach the defences. Thus began the long siege of Leningrad which lasted until 1944. Probably as many as one million Russians died in the siege, many of starvation. A hundred tonnes of food a day were needed to keep the city alive but this was hardly ever achieved. Most people lived on one tenth of the calorie intake needed to remain healthy. The sewage system was destroyed by bombing. There was no heating and no lighting, but the people of Leningrad held on.

Supplies being brought into Leningrad across the frozen Lake Ladoga.

Stalingrad

Meanwhile, Hitler planned to push south with a larger army, towards Stalingrad. Stalingrad was a sprawling, industrial city on the banks of the Volga river. Not only was it industrial but it was a centre for communications along the huge river and a major road junction. It was close to the Caucasus, an area where major Russian oilfields lay. The Germans were keen to capture these for themselves.

The city was also important for another reason. It was named after Stalin, the leader of the Soviet Union, because he had taken part in defending it during the Russian Civil War. Stalin did not want the city to fall to the Germans. He ordered that it must be held at all costs. For his part, Hitler knew that if he could take Stalingrad it would be a crushing blow to the Russians.

By the night of 23 August, the German armies had reached Rostov and the Russians were fast running out of places into which to retreat. From this time Stalingrad was under constant air attack. Hitler had decided to concentrate his forces on taking Stalingrad rather than the oilfields in the Caucasus. This was against the advice of his army commanders, but by this time Hitler had sacked his commander-in-chief. He assumed the position himself, and was intent on taking all the military decisions. The Germans encircled the city so that the only way in and out for the Russians was across the river to the east bank.

Fierce fighting

Through the late summer and early autumn, the fighting became fiercer in the city itself. Street by street, house by house, cellar by cellar the Germans and Russians fought for possession of the city. On 14 September, the central station changed hands four times. In October, the Russians were able to bring heavier guns to fire on the Germans from the east bank. By now the Germans knew they were running out of time. The Russian winter was approaching and the Russians were planning a counter-attack.

On 19 November, the Russians counter-attacked. They ripped into the German defences. In the following weeks, the Russians encircled the German army under General Paulus. Hitler would not allow him to retreat and to encourage Paulus he made him a Field Marshal. Hitler also ordered supplies to be flown in to the trapped German army. But more than this was needed, and on 31 January 1943 Paulus and the remains of the German army surrendered.

The cost to Germany

It is difficult to know exact figures, but Stalingrad may have cost the Germans one-and-a-half-million men, dead, wounded, missing or taken prisoner. This was about one quarter of all the soldiers they had in Russia. It was a huge loss for Germany and an even bigger defeat. It was the beginning of the end for their campaign in Russia, and for the Russians it was a glimmer of hope.

The world map on pages 44–45 shows the Soviet Union and Stalingrad.

Battle raged day and night in the ruined city of Stalingrad. Soviet and German soldiers fought over every house.

BATTLE FACTS
THE LIFE EXPECTANCY OF A RUSSIAN SOLDIER IN STALINGRAD WAS 24 HOURS.

OF 110,000 GERMANS TAKEN PRISONER, 5 PER CENT SURVIVED

The Battle of Kursk 1943

The city of Kursk lies 450 kilometres south of Moscow. It is surrounded by rolling plains, rivers and woods. In July 1943 the Germans and Russians faced each other over a long front line. Around Kursk the front line bulged westwards because the Russians had taken more land. This bulge in a front line is called a 'salient'. The Germans planned to cut this salient in half. They called the battle plan 'Citadel'.

The Germans began to assemble a huge army with many tanks and guns. The Russians knew about their plans because they could see the German build-up, but also because some of the senior German officers who were opposed to Hitler sent information to a spy ring based in Switzerland. This information was then forwarded to the Russians. Furthermore, the Russians had been building more and more tanks, aircraft and guns in their factories in the east. They had been training more and more soldiers and had received American supplies, sent from Britain by the Royal Navy to northern Russian ports. They also built trenches and put in minefields around important parts of the salient.

T34 tanks took Russian troops into the attack.

Beginning of the Battle of Kursk, 5 July 1943

In fact the Russians did not wait for the Germans to attack. At 2 a.m. on 5 July, the Russian artillery opened fire on the surprised Germans. The Battle of Kursk had begun. The German armies attacked on each side of the salient and broke through to the south. The fighting often went on all day and through the night.

By 11 July the Germans were near Prokhorovka and were closing in. The Russians were throwing in everything to stop them. On 12 July, the Russian General Rotmistrov was ordered to attack. He had about 900 tanks against about the same number of German tanks. It was the biggest tank battle of World War Two. But air attacks, rocket battery fire and artillery attacks continued too. Despite huge Russian losses, the battle turned against the Germans. At this time, Hitler heard that the **Allies** (the Americans and British) had landed in Italy so he withdrew some of the German army from Kursk to fight in Italy. The Russians counter-attacked and drove the Germans back.

Soviet women fighters

Of the twelve million front-line soldiers in the Soviet armed forces during World War Two, one million were women. There were women pilots in their own air regiments, with women mechanics and ground crew.

There were women tank commanders, snipers and soldiers in addition to women working in the more traditional support roles of doctors, nurses, ambulance drivers, munitions, farm and office workers.

Soviet tanks and soldiers

The Germans were amazed that, however great the Russian losses, there were always fresh soldiers, more tanks, aeroplanes and guns. They were also surprised by the quality of the Russian tanks. These tanks were built, in the east, at a huge factory in a place called Tankograd. The most popular tank was the T34. Apart from heavy armour, a powerful diesel engine and a large gun, it had wide tracks which made it very good across rough country. The armoured body was sloped rather than square, so that at least some shells slid past it. But more than anything it was reliable and easy to maintain on the battlefield.

The Germans were also surprised by the quality of the soldiers themselves, who were far tougher and better trained than the soldiers that the Germans had met when they first invaded the Soviet Union. By 1943 Russia was geared up for war.

From this time on, the Germans never won another significant battle in Russia – or indeed in the whole war.

*By the winter of 1943, Soviet women in the Night Bomber Regiment were flying up to fifteen combat **sorties** a night in freezing conditions, in open planes carrying 300 kilos of bombs.*

The Mediterranean Sea

The defeat of France in June 1940 changed the whole picture around the Mediterranean Sea. Mussolini, the Italian leader and Hitler's ally, saw an opportunity to gain more land in Africa and in 1940 decided to attack British possessions in North Africa.

By December, the British were fighting back. British and Australian forces took 130,000 Italian prisoners and regained control in North Africa. (See page 34). Victories in East Africa followed and Britain felt more sure of control of the eastern Mediterranean. However, this confidence was soon shaken when in April 1941 Germany reinforced and replaced Italy in the fighting in south-east Europe. By mid–1941 Germany had control of all of south-east Europe around the Mediterranean.

The importance of the Mediterranean Sea

The Mediterranean was vital to both sides. Loss of the use of the Mediterranean would cut off Britain from the oilfields of the Middle East and contact with India. In addition, at some future date, Britain might be able to invade German-dominated Europe from North Africa.

The invasion of Europe by the Allies from Africa, the Soviet Union and Britain, starting in 1943, culminated in the defeat of Germany in 1945.

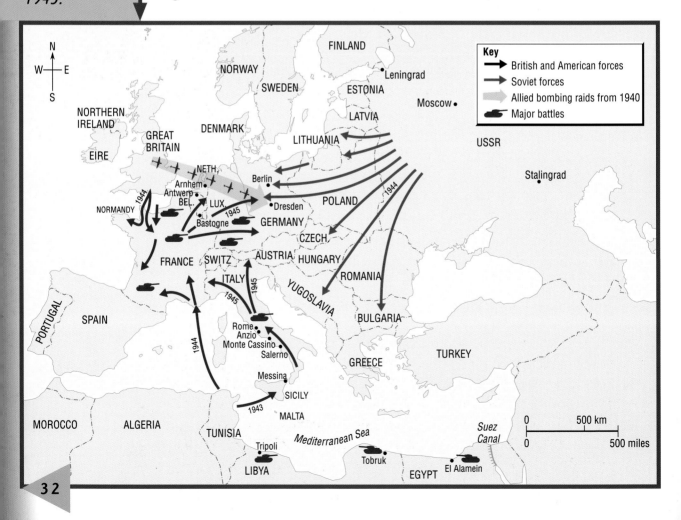

Rommel in North Africa

With this in view, Hitler sent Erwin Rommel to North Africa in the spring of 1941. He was a gifted strategist and a great leader. He was soon driving the British back through Libya towards Egypt, despite reinforcements of Indian, Australian, New Zealand and South African soldiers. By 11 April, the Australian 9th Division was surrounded by Rommel at Tobruk.

A column of German prisoners captured by the Allies during their conquest of Tunisia in 1943.

Meanwhile, Britain was more successful in the Middle East. Communications with the Soviet Union were maintained and Britain's supply routes to the oilfields and via the Gulf to India and the east were secured. Confidence in support from these areas was shaken, however, when Japan entered the war and devastated the British position in south-east Asia.

The entry of Japan into the war in December 1941 meant that many British Commonwealth soldiers went to fight on that front rather than in North Africa. Thus although the British forces, renamed the Eighth Army, chased Rommel 500 kilometres back to Tripoli, they did not defeat him. In early summer 1942, Rommel obtained more supplies and counter-attacked. This time the British were driven right back to Egypt, losing Tobruk on the way. The Germans were triumphant. The British base at Malta was almost put out of action, and German **U-boats** and aircraft severely damaged British **convoys** in the Mediterranean in August 1942. However, the British held on under their new commander, Montgomery, and Rommel got no further.

Tanks in the desert

Both the Germans and British understood that tanks and guns were the dominant weapons in the open, sandy deserts of North Africa. The British used their own Crusader tanks and American Stuart tanks, but the light armour of both was inferior to the German tank armour and meant that the Germans won more tank-versus-tank battles.

The Battle of El Alamein 1942

On 22 June 1942, Hitler promoted Rommel to Field Marshal. Now opposing him in North Africa was the British General Montgomery in command of the Eighth Army. Montgomery's first order was that the Eighth Army would not retreat any further. It would hold the line at Alam Halfa. The line was about 65 kilometres long, running from the sea to the Qattara Depression. It was least strongly held in the south. However, despite an attack by Rommel in August, the line held and Montgomery carried on reorganizing his army. He refused to be pressed by the British government or anyone else to attack Rommel until he was sure he had the means to defeat him.

Field Marshal Erwin Rommel (on the left) led the German campaign in North Africa.

He was also helped by the '**Enigma**' code-breaker, which told the British exactly where Rommel's supply ships were. Sixty per cent of German shipping was sunk before it reached North Africa.

During September and October reinforcements arrived, including 300 American Sherman tanks. By 23 October, Montgomery was ready. He had 230,000 men and 1030 tanks. This was against Rommel's 100,000 men and 500 tanks. The British also had air superiority.

The battle – 23 October–4 November 1942

The British started fighting at night with an attack from their heavy guns. Then the soldiers attacked. The fighting was fierce as the Germans threw in their tanks to stem the British attack. Rommel, who had been on sick leave in Italy, flew back to take command on 25 October. Much of the fighting took place along the coastal strip where both sides had their supply lines. One hard-fought battle was for control of Kidney Hill, which the British gained. They then used heavy artillery before launching into a tank battle with the Germans. After the battle, the Germans had only 35 working tanks left and Rommel decided to withdraw. (For Alamein, see map page 32).

Hitler ordered him to stay where he was but this was futile as the British broke through the German lines on 4 November and started to sweep west. Rommel ordered a full retreat towards Tobruk.

The pursuit

Montgomery stopped to reorganize his army and then set off after the Germans. He hoped to encircle them on the coast and force them to surrender, but Rommel did not intend to be trapped like that and, helped by bad weather, retreated along the coast. Montgomery realized it would be a long chase. For the next three months the British pursued the Germans for 2250 kilometres along the coast of North Africa. The going was often slow, as booby traps and an increasing number of German prisoners slowed up the British.

Rommel reached the border of Tunisia on 4 February 1943. Although Montgomery had not defeated Rommel, he had pushed the Germans right back. The Eighth Army had suffered 13,500 casualties in the Battle of El Alamein and Rommel had lost nearly all his tanks. The Germans, with the Italians, held out in Tunisia until May 1943 when they were decisively defeated by British and American forces. By this time, Rommel himself had been invalided out so he did not see the surrender of 125,000 German and nearly as many Italian soldiers to the **Allies**.

With North Africa clear, the way was open for the Americans and British to invade Italy.

General Montgomery watches his troops in action from the turret of his tank during the North African campaign.

BATTLE FACTS:
BATTLE OF EL ALAMEIN – 23 OCTOBER–4 NOVEMBER 1942

SEPT/OCT	ROMMEL ORDERS 500,000 MINES TO BE LAID
23/24 OCT	ARTILLERY AND AIR BOMBARDMENT
24 OCT	BRITISH ADVANCE HELD UP BY MINEFIELDS
31 OCT	BRITISH CUT THE COAST ROAD
2 NOV	FIERCE FIGHTING FOR KIDNEY HILL
3 NOV	HITLER COUNTERMANDS ROMMEL'S ORDER TO WITHDRAW
4 NOV	BRITISH BREAK THROUGH ROMMEL'S LINES

Italy and the Far East

Early in 1943 the Germans and Italians were forced out of North Africa. The British and Americans turned their attention to Italy (see map p. 32).

(see map p. 32)

On 10 July the **Allies** landed in Sicily, and by 17 August they had fought their way across the island to Messina. After this they faced the problems of landing on the mainland of Italy. Mussolini, the Italian leader, was forcibly deposed and the new Italian government considered making peace with the Allies. However, the Germans decided to reinforce Italy so that when the Allies landed they met fierce resistance.

The challenge of Italy

The Italian **peninsula** is long, narrow and mountainous, and the rivers run across it. Not only does an invading army have to fight through mountains, which are easy to defend, they have to cross large rivers, which are also easy to defend.

The Americans wanted to concentrate on north-west Europe, where the plan was to land a huge force of soldiers which would fight their way to Germany and so defeat Hitler. What they did not want was a long-drawn-out battle in Italy, which would take away manpower and weapons from France. The British argued that Italy was the 'soft underbelly' of Europe and was an easier way to reach Germany than across heavily defended France. The Americans agreed to carry on.

The ruins of the monastery of Monte Cassino in 1944, after months of attack by Allied troops. The monastery was originally founded in 529.

Monte Cassino

The Allies fought their way to Naples and undertook landings along the coast at Salerno and Anzio. They took Naples on 1 October. The mountains, the winter weather and torrential rain held up the Allies and gave the Germans time to build defences. Field Marshal Albert Kesselring was in charge of German defences. He decided to stop the Allies just south of Rome at the Garigliano Valley. The line the Germans held was

called the Gustav Line. Mountains rose above the valley to the north. At the western end, the River Liri cut a path through, providing a route to Rome. On the corner, overlooking both valleys and therefore dominating the route north to Rome, sat the monastery fortress of Monte Cassino. The Allies decided they must take it.

The battle began in January 1944 and by February Allied soldiers were within 400 metres of the monastery, but they could get no further and suffered heavy losses. Down to a quarter of their strength, they were relieved by Indian divisions. A programme of bombing began, followed by an attack by the New Zealand Corps. More attacks followed but, despite heavy casualties, Monte Cassino held out. The final battle for the monastery started on 11 May. On 18 May, Polish soldiers took the now empty shell of Monte Cassino. The Gustav Line was broken. Rome fell on 4 June 1944.

The Allies fight on

Fighting went on in Italy until well into 1945. This meant the Germans had to keep soldiers (25 divisions) fighting there which they could have used in Russia or to defend northern Europe. It also gave the Allies a great deal of experience in landing large numbers of soldiers, tanks and weapons from the sea onto well-defended beaches. This stood them in good stead for D-Day.

The Far East

Meanwhile, in the Far East, British forces were fighting to keep Japan out of India. After three months of fighting, the British defeated the Japanese at Imphal and started to retake Burma.

The jeep was one of the most ingenious vehicles. It could negotiate rocky hills, marshy swamps and shifting sands. The jeep was designed for messenger service, but was soon used on every front from Russia to Italy, by anyone who could drive, for everything from evacuating wounded to towing guns.

Orde Wingate and the Chindits

Orde Wingate was an unusual British soldier. He organized a guerrilla group of British, Gurkha and Burmese soldiers, called the Chindits, to fight behind Japanese lines in Burma in 1943. He not only led the Chindits, but helped to train a similar US force. He was killed in a plane crash in March 1944.

The Battle of the Beaches 1944

By 1944 the **Allies** were ready to invade German-held western Europe. The base from which they planned to do this was Britain, so for months American and Canadian soldiers poured across the Atlantic together with tanks, guns and aeroplanes.

Operation Overlord

The invasion was code-named Overlord and it was planned for June 1944 when the weather should be fairly good. It was very important that the place at which the Allies would land was kept secret. The obvious place to cross the Channel was at the narrowest part, across the Straits of Dover, and this was where the Germans had most of their troops. In fact, the Allies chose Normandy.

Allied troops landing on a Normandy beach on D-Day, 6 June 1944.

The Allies used about 7000 ships, of which 4000 carried soldiers and weapons to land on the beaches. The other 3000 were either to bombard the Germans from the sea or to carry supplies such as food, ammunition and medicine. The Allies also needed harbours. Since the big ships could not sail up to the beaches, huge artificial harbours, known as 'Mulberries', were built. These were then towed across the Channel to Normandy. An ingenious underwater oil pipe was also built, code-named Pluto.

D-Day 1944

On 6 June 1944, the Allied invasion began. The weather was bad. Hundreds of soldiers felt seasick as they headed for Normandy. Each soldier had enough food to last him for 24 hours, French money and his pack. Thousands of ships sailed through the night covered by thousands of aeroplanes. The best-planned invasion ever was under way. It was like moving the whole of a large city to France in one day.

The beaches were defended with mines, barbed wire and wooden obstacles in the water. Major General Hobart of the 79th Armoured Division thought up different ways of getting through the German defences, including minesweeping tanks and bridge-laying tanks.

The landings were made on five beaches, which had code names. Sword, Juno and Gold were British and Canadian beaches. Omaha and Utah were American beaches. During the night paratroopers had been dropped to attack German guns. By early morning, the Allied ships were coming up to the beaches. The soldiers rushed ashore while the large ships bombarded the German guns. The Americans had a difficult landing on Omaha. There were cliffs defended by the best German troops along the coast. However, after losses of about 3000 soldiers, the beach at Omaha was taken.

General Eisenhower talking to American paratroopers on D–Day as they prepare to take off for the invasion of France.

By the end of the first day, the Allies had landed 156,000 men on the five beaches and they were not going to be pushed back into the sea. The next day the Mulberry harbours were put in place and then the big ships could tie up and unload their cargoes of tanks and lorries to support the invading army. One of the Mulberries was immediately destroyed by a storm, but the other one remained intact.

Onwards to Germany

D–Day was just the first day of the invasion. It took weeks of bitter fighting to push the Germans back. Day after day more soldiers were landed on the Normandy beaches until the Allies captured ports and could use proper harbours to land men and supplies. By August the Allies had fought their way to Paris. By September they hoped to cross the Rhine.

D–Day was vitally important. If the Germans had pushed the Allied soldiers off the beaches that day the course of the war would have changed dramatically. It is unlikely that the Germans could have won, but the Russians could have made peace on their own terms without consulting the Americans and British.

FORCES AVAILABLE ON D-DAY

	GERMAN	ALLIES
FRONT-LINE FORCES	580,000	156,000
RESERVES	850,000	2,000,000

THE ALLIES HAD KEPT THE SECRET OF WHERE THEY WOULD LAND SO WELL THAT THE GERMANS COULD NOT CONCENTRATE ALL THEIR FRONT-LINE FORCES IN TIME TO DRIVE THE ALLIES BACK INTO THE SEA.

The Battle of the Bulge 1944–45

RAF air and ground crew in front of a Lancaster bomber. Bombers were used to bomb Germany directly and to support the advancing Allied forces. By this stage of the war, the Allies had the manpower, the fuel and the equipment to

The **Allies** landed in Normandy on 6 June 1944 and then had to fight their way to Germany. It was not easy. Hitler knew the Allies needed enormous amounts of supplies for their armies. All these had to come from their base in Britain across the English Channel. Therefore Hitler ordered that all the French Channel ports must be held. So Le Havre, Boulogne, Calais and Dunkirk were held like fortresses. This meant that however far east the Allies got, they still had to truck all their supplies from Normandy. This slowed up their advance.

On 4 September, the Allies took the port of Antwerp. This should have helped them as big ships could come into Antwerp. However, Hitler had ordered that the fortress further out at the mouth of the river be held at all costs. So although the Allies held Antwerp, if ships tried to sail up the river to it they would be blown up. It took the Allies until 28 November to open the river. All this time they were short of supplies such as petrol and could not drive forward. It was at this point that Hitler decided to attack.

The weather was bad so that the Allied planes could neither see nor bomb the German forces. Moreover the Allies were not expecting the Germans to attack in the hilly part of Belgium, and since the Germans kept radio silence, the Allies had not been able to listen in to coded German army orders and work out what was happening.

The Germans attack

The Germans struck on 16 December, to the intense surprise of the Americans. The US troops fought bravely but were overwhelmed. The Germans rushed on. But the Americans reacted quickly. There was fierce fighting around the village of Bastogne. The Americans were asked to surrender but refused and fought on. The weather improved on 23 December and the Americans and British fought back with aeroplanes as well as soldiers. By now their ships were arriving at the port of Antwerp so they had plenty of supplies for the soldiers. The Germans were running out of petrol. They had failed to capture an Allied petrol dump.

The 'Bulge'

In early January, the British and American forces attacked the 'bulge' in the German lines. They cut through and by 8 January the Germans were surrendering. This was the end of what became known as the Battle of the Bulge.

Two German foot soldiers pass by a burning tank during the Battle of the Bulge.

The Germans had 100,000 casualties to the Allies' 76,000. But they had not only lost soldiers, they had lost 600 tanks and 1600 aircraft. At this stage of the war they could not afford to lose so much. They delayed the Allies on their way to conquer Germany by about six weeks. However, it was obvious that this would be their last real attempt to stop the Allies reaching Germany.

The Germans were collapsing but the fighting went on for months as the Allies fought their way into Germany. The Germans blew up bridges over rivers as they retreated so Allied engineers had to build bridges to get their soldiers across. This took time. Meanwhile the Russians were advancing on Germany from the east. In fact most of the German army was fighting the Russians in the east.

On 25 April 1945, the Russian and the Allied advance troops met on the River Elbe and shook hands. Meanwhile other Russian forces had reached Berlin, and to avoid capture, Hitler committed suicide on 30 April. Germany surrendered a week later, and the war in Europe was over.

There is a world map on which you can find the Battle of the Bulge on pages 44–45.

> **ODDS IN THE ALLIES' FAVOUR**
> MILITARY EXPERTS ESTIMATE THAT AN ATTACKER NEEDS A SUPERIORITY OVER A DEFENDER OF 3:1 TO BE SUCCESSFUL. BY 1945, THE ALLIES HAD A SUPERIORITY OVER THE GERMANS OF 10:1.

The end – the fight for the Pacific

After the Battle of Midway in June 1942, the Americans began to work their way towards Japan. Fighting alongside Australian forces in the South West Pacific Ocean they eventually secured New Guinea. New Guinea lies close to Australia and it was important to hold it so the Japanese could not invade Australia.

After New Guinea, the **Allies** fought for island after island. All the time they were trying to push the Japanese back towards Japan itself. Often the fighting was very fierce because the Japanese were brave soldiers who had been brought up never to surrender. It took until February 1943 to clear the jungle island of Guadalcanal.

US marines display Japanese flags captured during the battle for Iwo Jima.

Throughout 1943, both the Americans and the Japanese worked to strengthen their grip on the islands they held. But the advantage had tipped towards the Americans. There were three main reasons for this. The Americans were now making huge numbers of new ships. In 1943 alone, they made more ships than the whole Japanese navy had at the beginning of the war. Second, the Japanese were losing more planes and aircrews than they could make or train. The Americans were making more and more planes and training more and more pilots. Third, although it had taken the Americans six months to capture Guadalcanal, they had done it in the end and shown that Japan could be defeated.

The fighting went on. The Americans took to island hopping. Sometimes they left an island to the Japanese and went on to the next one. All the time they were heading for Japan itself. Far from getting tired of the war as the Japanese hoped, the Americans were becoming more determined that nothing less than the total defeat of Japan would do.

To Okinawa and Hiroshama

By mid-1944, America was thinking in terms of invading Japan. But how was this to be done? Aeroplanes were enormously important. They were needed to protect ships carrying soldiers to invade and they were needed to bomb the enemy. America needed airbases within reach of Japan. Both America and Japan knew that the islands of Iwo Jima and Okinawa were important. American planes could fly from these islands to bomb Japan and to protect an invasion fleet.

First, the Americans took the small volcanic island of Iwo Jima 1300 kilometres from Japan. Then they invaded Okinawa, which is only 600 kilometres from Japan. They bombarded the island from ships for several weeks. The Japanese countered this with kamikaze attacks. They filled old planes with bombs and taught young pilots to fly them. The pilots flew straight into the American and British ships like human bombs – these were suicide missions. One US sailor said that the deck of his aircraft carrier rumpled up like a banana skin as the entire plane landed and exploded.

Australian soldiers coming ashore from landing craft during the Pacific campaign, where they fought closely with the Americans.

The invasion went ahead on 1 April 1945. It was Easter Sunday. The Japanese fought hard and it took over two months to take the whole of Okinawa. It was a very important victory. The Americans brought in their big bombers and could now reach Tokyo, the capital of Japan. They were getting nearer to invading Japan, but Okinawa made one other thing clear. The Japanese had lost nine men for every American lost. They would fight for Japan to the death. If America invaded Japan, it might mean the deaths of a million or more Allied soldiers. It was this fear that led the Allies to decide to use the atom bomb on Hiroshima on 6 August 1945 and on Nagasaki on 9 August. Japan surrendered and the world war was over.

THE COST OF OKINAWA	
JAPANESE LOSSES	110,000 SOLDIERS AND OVER 110,000 CIVILIANS DEAD
ALLIED LOSSES	50,000 DEAD AND WOUNDED

A world at war – a map of main battles

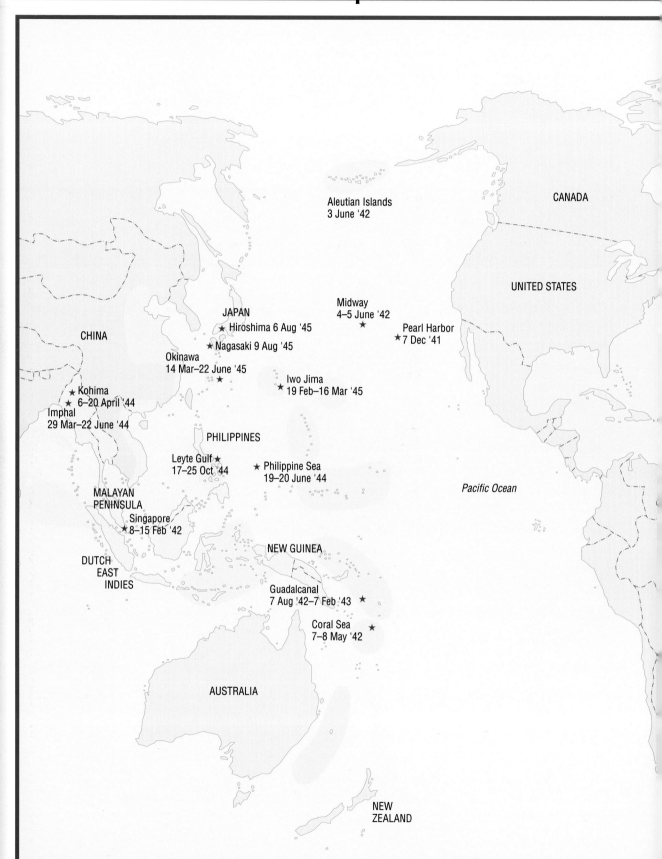

Aleutian Islands
3 June '42

CANADA

UNITED STATES

JAPAN

Midway
4–5 June '42 ★

Pearl Harbor
★ 7 Dec '41

CHINA

★ Hiroshima 6 Aug '45

★ Nagasaki 9 Aug '45

Okinawa
14 Mar–22 June '45

Iwo Jima
★ 19 Feb–16 Mar '45

★ Kohima
★ 6–20 April '44

Imphal
29 Mar–22 June '44

PHILIPPINES

Leyte Gulf ★

★ Philippine Sea
19–20 June '44

Pacific Ocean

MALAYAN
PENINSULA

Singapore
★ 8–15 Feb '42

DUTCH
EAST
INDIES

NEW GUINEA

Guadalcanal
7 Aug '42–7 Feb '43 ★

Coral Sea
7–8 May '42 ★

AUSTRALIA

NEW
ZEALAND

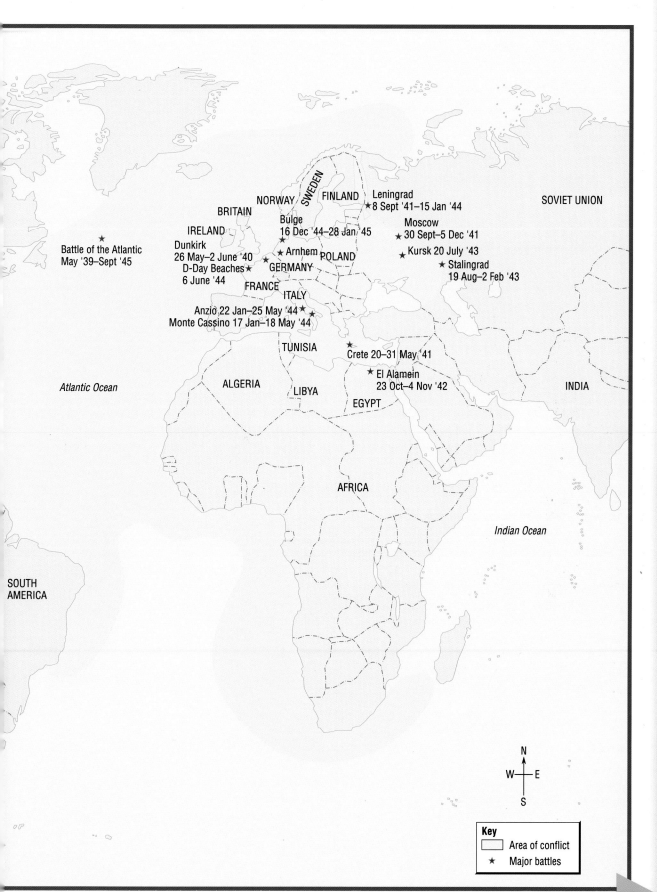

NORWAY
SWEDEN
FINLAND
BRITAIN
Bulge
16 Dec '44–28 Jan '45
Leningrad
★ 8 Sept '41–15 Jan '44
SOVIET UNION
IRELAND
Moscow
★ 30 Sept–5 Dec '41
Dunkirk
26 May–2 June '40
★ Arnhem
POLAND
★ Kursk 20 July '43
Battle of the Atlantic
May '39–Sept '45
★
D-Day Beaches ★
6 June '44
GERMANY
★ Stalingrad
19 Aug–2 Feb '43
FRANCE
ITALY
Anzio 22 Jan–25 May '44 ★
Monte Cassino 17 Jan–18 May '44
★
TUNISIA
Crete 20–31 May '41 ★
Atlantic Ocean
ALGERIA
LIBYA
★ El Alamein
23 Oct–4 Nov '42
EGYPT
INDIA
AFRICA
Indian Ocean
SOUTH
AMERICA

N
W—E
S

Key
☐ Area of conflict
★ Major battles

World War Two timeline

Year	Western Europe	Russian Front	Mediterranean/ North Africa	Far East
1939	1 Sept: Germany invades Poland 3 Sept: Britain at war			
1940	Dunkirk, Battle of Britain			
1941		Germany invades USSR		Pearl Harbor
1942		Aug: Stalingrad Leningrad besieged	Oct–Nov: El Alamein	Feb: Singapore April: Philippines May: Coral Sea June: Midway
1943		Feb: Stalingrad July: Kursk	10 July Allies invade Italy via Sicily	
1944	June: D-Day	Jan: siege of Leningrad ends	May: Monte Cassino	April: Kohima May–June: Imphal
1945	May: Germany surrenders			Feb–May: Iwo Jima Mar–June: Okinawa Aug: Hiroshima Nagasaki Japan surrenders

Further reading and places of interest

Further reading

The Home Front, History of Britain Topic Book, Heinemann Library, 1995

The Blitz, History of Britain Topic Book Heinemann Library, 1995

Hiroshima, Turning Points in History, Richard Tames, Heinemann Library, 1998

Pearl Harbor, Turning Points in History, Richard Tames, Heinemann Library, 1998

Adolf Hitler, Profiles, Richard Tames, Heinemann Library, 1998

Women's War, Fiona Reynoldson, Wayland, 1991

Prisoners of War, Fiona Reynoldson, Wayland, 1991

Women and War, Fiona Reynoldson, Wayland, 1993

Sources

History of the Twentieth Century, Vol. II, Martin Gilbert, 1999

Times Historical Atlas of World War II

Novels

Children of the Blitz, Robert Westall, Macmillan, 1995

The Dolphin Crossing, Jill Paton Walsh, Puffin, 1995

A Spoonful of Jam, Michelle Magorian, Mammoth, 1998

The Machine Gunners, Robert Westall, Macmillan, 1994

A Time of Fire, Robert Westall, Macmillan, 1995

World War Two websites

World War Two:
   www.bbc.co.uk/history/wwtwo.shtml

Second World War Encyclopaedia:
   www.spartacus.schoolnet.co.uk/zww.htm

The Imperial War Museum, London:
   www.iwm.org.uk/

Places of interest

Bovington Tank Museum, Dorset

Overlord Tapestry (D-Day), Portsmouth

RAF Museum, Duxford

local Regimental Museums (country-wide)

Imperial War Museum, London

Kent Battle of Britain Museum, Hawkinge, Kent

Glossary

Allies the British, French, Soviet Union (after June 1941) and USA (after December 1941)

appeasement to keep the peace by giving in to demands

Blitzkreig sudden, overwhelming attack

Bolsheviks political party in Russia that believed in communism. The Bolsheviks, led by Lenin, siezed power in Russia during the Russian Revolution in November 1917

chancellor chief minister

colony country that was taken over and run by another country

communist person believing in a classless society with all land and means of production owned by the state

convoy group travelling together, e.g. ships

Czechoslovakia country in central Europe bordering Germany to the east, which is now the Czech Republic and Slovakia

destroyer small, fast warship

dive bomber aeroplane that releases a bomb while diving

East Indies group of islands in the Far East (now Indonesia)

Enigma the Germans used Enigma machines to make codes for their armed forces to use

evacuation moving people to a place of safety

fascist person believing in extreme nationalism and restriction on individual freedom

glider troops soldiers who parachuted from gliders

Indo-China land in the Far East, including what is now called Vietnam, Cambodia and Laos

Lebensraum German word meaning 'living space'

Luftwaffe the German air force

Maginot Line line of forts built by France to stop a German attack

panzer name for a German armoured vehicle, often a tank

paratrooper soldier who parachutes from an aeroplane

peninsula a piece of land that is almost an island

pre-emptive attacking first to stop enemy action

radar use of high-powered radio pulses for locating objects. Radar stands for <u>ra</u>dio <u>d</u>etection <u>a</u>nd <u>r</u>anging.

reparations giving things to repair damage of some kind

sorties attacks

stock market place where stocks and shares are traded

treaty an agreement between countries

Treaty of Versailles treaty the victors made Germany sign at the end of World War One

tsar emperor (of Russia)

U-boat German submarine, short for *Unterseeboot*

Index